Tantric Reiki

Gail Radford

Tantric Reiki

Astrolog Publishing House

Cover Design: Na'ama Yaffe

© Astrolog Publishing House Ltd. 2005

ISBN 965-494-171-6

P. O. Box 1123, Hod Hasharon 45111, Israel
Tel: 972-9-7412044
Fax: 972-9-7442714

Astrolog Publishing House 2005

Welcome to a new world of transformational energy experiences. Through connection with and the uplifting of our beings' essential energies, we can attain sexual enlightenment and fulfillment entirely off the scale of what is usually possible for those of us in the modern Western world.

Reiki is a powerful technique in which the practitioner pulses energy toward his client (or himself) using a procedure which heals, uplifts, and connects a person to his higher and purer self. When reiki is directed purposely toward the sexual organs and/or when used before and during a sexual act performed according to the Tantric tradition, sex becomes a celebration of our most intense erotic potential. The Tantra is a collection of ancient spiritual guides which explain how sex can release powerful human energies which propel us to the infinite. Tantric Reiki can help move us far beyond any previously known sexual joy, making the act of sex a profound spiritual experience. The use of Reiki together with the Tantric sex teachings magnifies and glorifies the energy connection, allowing total surrender, peace, and ecstasy.

Let's journey now into the tantalizing knowledge that makes up Tantric Reiki. In order to arrive at a deep understanding of the process, we will explore its two elements, the Tantric Teachings, and Reiki individually, and subsequently together as Tantric Reiki.

Reiki

First, let's pronounce reiki correctly: *Ray'-Key*. The Japanese words for transfer and energy (*rei* and *ki*) combine to make up the concept of reiki.

Rei means "transcendence" or "free passage", and *ki* is the energy which makes up all that is. Therefore "transfer of energy" would be the simplest translation of the word. Indeed reiki does entail the movement of a person's essential energies both within his body and the transfer of energy from one to another. Let's take a look at this "energy" and examine what is meant by the term here.

Energy

All matter is made up of energy. This energy is sometimes called the Vital Life Force, or Universal Life Energy. This energy makes up our bodies, and even our minds. All of our emotions and feelings are movement of this energy on various frequencies. Low frequencies of vibrations make up negative or depressed states, while the highest bring us closest to nirvana or spiritual oneness with all that is. We are usually vulnerable to the influence of circumstances and events outside of ourselves, giving them the ability to raise or lower our energies according to what we observe, and subsequently feel. We may develop habitual thought patterns, though while negative, seem to ingrain themselves into our persons and are hard to release. These negative thoughts can block the natural healthy flow of energy through our systems and cause stress, illness, even death. The free movement of positive energy is essential for well-being and health of the physical body and the mind. When blockages are caused by stagnant or slow moving energy, ill effects of all kinds are suffered. Reiki is the art of causing vital free movement of the life energy in and around the body. It can release built up blockages, start the flow of life back up and keep it moving positively.

Reiki is usually thought of as a "healing art". It has the ability to regenerate the healthy functioning of all the body's organs and systems by balancing the energy flow. Reiki is a "hands-on" treatment. The practitioner applies his hands to the receiver (or to himself) and sends the healing energy through them. Reiki is not a belief system or set of theories, and does not rely on the faith of the receiver of the treatment. In fact, reiki works even at long distances and on recipients who are unaware that they are being sent a treatment. Likewise, reiki can successfully treat even a patient who does not believe in its efficacy. As the energy of the body comes into balance through reiki, the body releases illness and unwanted patterns of behavior. The vibrational frequency of the person is raised as the reiki accomplishes its task.

The Story of Reiki

The absolute origin of reiki is obscured by history. It is believed that a system of energy healing which consisted of sounds and symbols was used in Tibet over two thousand years ago. Other cultures have developed similar energy healing disciplines, but we have no way of knowing which of them was the direct precursor of what is now known as reiki.

Reiki is now enjoying a robust revival around the world. This revival has its roots in Japan, over a century ago, with a certain physician and educator, Dr. Mikao Usui, who reintroduced reiki to the modern world through an amazing series of events. A devout Christian born in Japan, Usui believed unquestioningly in the Holy Scriptures and in Jesus Christ as savior. The stories of Christ's ability to heal fascinated him. Usui had a burning desire to understand by what power Christ had carried out his miracles of healing. He wondered what source held the mighty curative force into which Christ had tapped to perform his wonders. The question nagged at him so fiercely that he set out on a tireless quest for answers.

Usui embarked upon a systematic study of the great spiritual leaders throughout history. Traveling to the United States in the late 19th century, Usui tried to find the answers among his Christian teachers there. This proved futile, however, and he returned to Japan, with the idea of studying the healing powers of the Buddha, who also had performed medical miracles by use of mysterious divine powers. The monks he interviewed could provide no satisfactory answer to his queries however, leaving him as frustrated and curious as before. He still felt certain that the powers accessed by Jesus and the Buddha were still in existence and that by understanding them man could avail himself of healing whenever he wished.

Usui continued his exhaustive quest, arriving at a secluded monastery where the abbot was intrigued by Usui's questions. He invited the Christian to remain in the monastery and provided him ancient Japanese and Chinese texts to study. And study Usui did, still finding no answers, even after he learned Sanskrit and pored over the ancient Tibetan Sutras.

Dr. Usui decided to take a trip to northern India, where, he was told, there were some ancient scrolls found in the Himalayas which contained rare information. On his return from this journey Usui declared that he had found the answer to his question, or at least, an intellectual answer. Finally he felt he had progressed closer to the truth he was seeking. But the power to actually heal still remained illusive, contained as it was in the divine, and inaccessible to mere mortals.

Usui asked the abbot how he could infuse his new intellectual understanding with the spark of the divine, which would enable him to heal as the great masters had done. Dr. Usui was instructed to climb the holy mountain of Kurama, near Kyoto and to fast and meditate for a period of twenty-one days. This he did, sitting on a mountain pinnacle, earnestly praying and waiting for inspiration.

On the twenty first night, the inky sky was suddenly illuminated with a bright light which as he watched, drew nearer and nearer. Usui sat mesmerized by the sight of the strange light. He was afraid, but somehow knew that the light was the sign he'd prayed for, so he did not flee. All at once the light flew quickly toward him, striking him in the forehead so mightily that he thought he was surely dying. Still alive, he lay entranced by visions. He saw tiny lights and colors dancing in his head, and bubbles containing shapes and symbols. Intuition told him these images contained a vital message, and he committed the characters to memory before they vanished.

When this vision receded, Dr. Usui knew he had just received a precious gift. He ecstatically ran down the mountain as the sun rose on the twenty second day feeling full of vigor and not at all like a man who had not eaten for three weeks time. This was the first miracle, and the miracles continued in that fashion. He accidentally wounded his foot during his descent from the pinnacle, but in an instant the bleeding and pain were curbed. Sign after sign showed him that he had indeed crossed the threshold into the secret world of healing powers. Stopping at an inn for a meal, Usui healed the innkeeper's daughter of a hideous tooth infection. Returning to the monastery he cured one of the monks of rheumatism by laying his hands on the painful areas.

Joyfully, Usui began to use his powers at every possible turn. He healed people from all walks of life who came to him with every possible human ailment. Gratified, he realized he finally had been given the powers and the answers he'd spent so many years seeking. Modern reiki was born!

Usui treated anyone who made his way to him and asked for a healing. He often refused payment for his services. Usui's story does not end there. After a while, Usui began to see repeat cases – those he had already healed were coming forth with new and more horrible hurts and weaknesses to be cured. Some of the very poor refused treatment, preferring to beg for sustenance than make the changes the reiki would help them manifest. He realized that his method would not give them anything but an immediate relief – and that what was needed was for the receiver of the healing to be a participant any cure which was to be lasting and meaningful. An active give and take was necessary between healer and patient in order for true change to take place in the energy body of the recipient of the cure. He saw that the nature and behavior of the people was what caused them to continue to fall ill, and that cure after cure was not a way out of their predicament. A fine tuning of the person's energy body was lacking, and without it, the healing would be temporary at best.

Meditating on all of this, Usui developed the Five Reiki Principles, and understanding of the characters which had been revealed to him in his original vision came clearly to his mind. He developed ways in which the recipient of the healing energy would take personal responsibility and change his life accordingly, thus keeping his vibrational frequency consistently higher than when the disease or ailment had occurred.

Principles of Reiki

Just for today, I will not be angry.
When we allow the emotion of anger to reside in our body and mind, we are functioning from a position of fear. By releasing the need to be angry, we come to realize there is nothing to fear. All is as it should be, and to push against what is by using anger is counterproductive.

Just for today, I will not worry.
Worry too, is a resistance to what we perceive. By allowing whatever is happening to be "okay" we also allow it to change to whatever we might desire to happen. The universe will give us what we imagine. Worry is usually a habitual imagining of the worse case scenario. If we continue to worry, the object of our fear will not disappoint us – it will appear! Therefore rather than worry about what we do not want to show up, we should direct our imaginations toward our desire.

Just for today, I will earn my living with honestly.
When we go about our daily tasks with honesty and integrity, while this may or may not impress our neighbors and coworkers, it has a profound effect on our own sense of self-worth. When we know, deep within ourselves that we are upright and worthy of esteem, we move through our lives with a calm happiness which begins to affect all that we encounter. Ripples of good energy emit from us which bring blessings of many kinds.

Just for today, I will give thanks for all that I have.
An attitude of gratitude is absolutely essential to the flow of positive energy within our beings. By focusing on what we already have that is life-giving and pleasing, we align our energy with these, and more of the same can flow into our experience. If instead, we focus on what we wish we had, our energies match that lack, and we simply attract more lack! By noticing and rejoicing over the wonders which have been bestowed on us, we allow abundance to flow toward us in every area of life. Every life, no matter how wretched it may seem, is full of blessings. To increase them they have only to be noticed and nurtured.

Just for today, I will love every creature and form of life
Our separateness from All That Is is an illusion. In actuality we are part of everything and everything is part of each of us. Therefore respect and love must be radiated at every other person and every other creature we encounter. Kindness showed a neighbor will be reflected back ten-fold. In this way we love and respect our very selves.

The Reiki Symbols

As part of the receiving of reiki through the divine revelation, Dr. Inui was given a set of powerful symbols which embody the reiki energy and allow its passage from one to another. By concentrating the energies, the symbols become repositories of healing. Each symbol contains the essence of healing in a particular area of human existence. This allows the practitioner to fine-tune the type of energies which are used in healing a particular person or ailment. The symbols strengthen the power of the reiki by becoming conduits for the quicker and more effective transmission of the energies.

1. Cho Ku Rei

The first symbol is that of the body. It is shaped roughly like a spiral turning in upon itself. The Cho Ku Rei is the symbol of power. It is used when strength is needed, or to purify spaces such as a home or vehicle. The Cho Ku Rei emits a powerful white light which charges the atmosphere with positive energy.

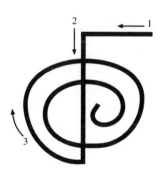

2. Sei Hei Ki

The second symbol is the symbol of feeling and thought. It is also called the symbol of emotional healing. Patterns of thought, which when entrenched can be called beliefs, are what drive our reality and thus it is vital that they be tuned to what we actually which to manifest. Our thoughts cause our emotions, and emotions are powerful creators of what happens to us in life. Old, obsolete, or 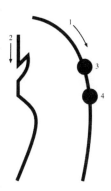 destructive thoughts and beliefs can and should be changed or eliminated. Reiki can be used to balance the emotions and rout out undesired thought patterns. Even childhood events and traumas which have affected us for years and seem difficult to release can be neutralized by the use of reiki, with the help of the second symbol. Many of our beliefs are held unconsciously, and even these can be brought to the surface for release when this is in our best interest. We may believe certain "truths", but on examination we realize that many of these are only perceptions which can be changed, bringing about pro-found positive change in our lives. We may limit ourselves or have negative ideas as to our potential and worth, but with the proper reiki treatment these perceptions can be brought to light and more appropriate beliefs can take their places. These changes sometimes happen with out the necessity for conscious thought or intent for them to happen.

The second symbol can also be used to improve memory, to curb bad habits and addictions, and to increase understanding and learning power.

3. Hon Hash Hez Venosh

The name of the third reiki symbol means "The god that is in me blesses the god that is in you for healing and enlightenment". This is the symbol of spirit. Used for reiki treatment when the recipient is a long distance from the practitioner. It knows no limits in space and time and can reach its destination under any condition. The third symbol can even be sent into the past and future, readjusting a person's karmic

make-up and healing events that may have occurred in another plane. When one is nervous about the outcome of a future event, the Hon Hash Hez Venosh can be sent out ahead to even out the energies and create a welcoming and conducive energetic environment for success. Since physical contact with the recipient is not necessary when using this symbol, it can be used to treat ailments where touch would be dangerous as in the case of open wounds and burns.

4. Dai Ku Meo

This symbol vibrates at a very high frequency and is able to bring about speedy, sometimes immediate, healing. The Dai Ku Meo lends a greater unity and fullness to the reiki treatment. By bringing the divine down to the physical plane, this symbol infuses the healer

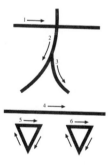

and the patient with wisdom and blessings. Its action is extremely powerful and usually not used by any but the most experienced reiki masters.

5. Zonar

The fifth reiki symbol is able to work from the present, reaching far into the past. It heals traumas sustained in previous lifetimes, and clears up "bad karma". Useful for the treatment of adults still suffering from childhood abuse or neglect, it reaches back in time and deep into the subconscious mind.

6. Harthi

The Harthi, the sixth reiki symbol, is a pyramid shape with a cross in the center. It contains the energies of love, beauty, harmony, and truth. Problems concerning the heart or emotions connected to the giving and receiving of love are healed by this symbol. Relationship woes, such as strife within families or couples, generation gap problems, and sibling rivalry are helped by this symbol. The symbol fosters an understanding of the unity of All That Is, and that we are truly one with one another. Compassion for one another and empathy with the pain of others are natural to us, but sometimes our ability to connect with them is blocked. This symbol clears the blockage and lets the love flow.

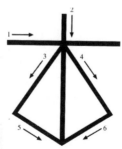

7. Halu

The seventh reiki symbol is a stronger version of the fifth, the zonar. It restores balance to mental, physical and emotional systems. It allows the mind to tap into deeply held and suppressed traumas such as physical or sexual attacks. It releases karma and allows a higher awareness to come to the fore. Battered women, abused children, and other victims can benefit from the use of the halu together with the zonar for deep release of their traumas.

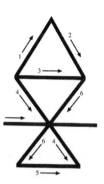

8. Rama

The eighth symbol connects the earthy plane with the spirit plane. It is used to cleanse a space of negative energy and allow the spiritual to enter. The rama grounds as well, providing a strong earth-heaven connection. It can also be used to provide protection, asserting a protective aura around people, places or objects to guard against injury, accidents, or theft.

9. Gnossa

The ninth symbol opens up the person to his or her higher awareness. Used before meditation, it can foster easier access to guides and inner knowing.

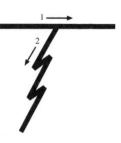

10. Eah Vah

The tenth reiki symbol aids in manifestation of our desires and in bringing desired projects and goals to fruition. This symbol has the ability to revive wilting plants. It jump-starts our aims and ambitions by connecting us to our ability to bring them to reality.

11. Shanti

The eleventh and final reiki symbol is useful for the release of fear. It exorcises useless anxiety from the mind, giving relief from nightmares and recurring irrational terrors. It induces a feeling of calm and security.

female   male

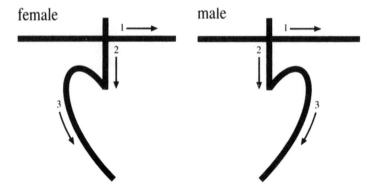

Who can perform reiki?

The secrets of reiki were passed by Dr. Usui to his most trusted students, the most notable of whom was Churjiro Hayashi. As Usui aged, Dr. Hayashi assumed more responsibility for the reiki clinic Usui had established in Tokyo, and ultimately took over its management. Hayashi passed on the knowledge to the next great reiki teacher, a Japanese – American woman who came to Hayashi for treatment in 1935, Takata. Takata was so taken by the power of reiki in her own cure that she undertook a thorough study of the discipline and received her "attunement" from Dr. Hayashi. Takata settled in the United States and introduced reiki to the Western World.

The ability to channel reiki is passed from teacher to student. Reiki is not a discipline that can be studied in books and learned by rote. It must be personally attained through "attunement", which is the passing of the energy between master and student. While other energy healing arts may use movement of energy and balancing of the energy centers in the body, only reiki channels the unique reiki energy received by Dr. Inui and passed from disciple to disciple.

At the attunement the reiki master draws the sacred reiki symbols in the air in front of the student. The student may or my not feel a powerful energy enter his body, and he may have visions of bright light or shapes. Whether or not he experiences these sensations however, the energy is transmitted, and he is able to use it to perform reiki on himself and others. Once a reiki master has made a student a reiki practitioner, the student's ability to channel reiki is permanent and complete. While he will never lose his ability to heal once attunement is complete, by practicing he becomes more sensitive and proficient. Since the days of Dr. Usui, hundreds and thousands of reiki masters have initiated their successors, and reiki has spread to all corners of the globe.

Attunement is received in several stages, or degrees. The student must be very serious about the desire to open himself to the receiving of reiki, for the attunement will allow him the precious ability to heal.

First degree reiki

The first degree begins with a tutorial about the history of reiki and an understanding of what it entails. At the first degree attunement the student is passed the 'ki' energy which is drawn into his body through the energy centers which we will describe below. The student's store of 'ki' is fully replenished and all blockages of its flow in his body are removed. The student is balanced mentally, spiritually, and emotionally. Aside from the tutorial, the actual energy attunement takes but a few moments. The master then instructs the student on the proper way to pass the energy to recipients by placing the hands correctly on the body. The newly attuned practitioner is now able to perform full body reiki on a recipient.

Second degree reiki

Once a reiki student has received first degree attunement he can progress at any time to the second degree. Usually he practices for a time and gains some experience before moving to the next level. It is suggested that a period of about three weeks be observed between attunements to allow the body to integrate the previous attunement. Since receiving the reiki energy can cause upheaval in the body and emotions, it's best to respect ones need for time to allow cleansing or changes that might be experienced. Moving too quickly to the next attunement could cause upheaval so uncomfortable as to be devastating in its effects.

Attunement to the second degree of reiki greatly increases the practitioner's ability to heal using the reiki energies. It is when being initiated into the second degree that the student begins to receive the powerful reiki symbols. He receives the first three symbols in the second degree – the symbols of body, emotion, and enlightenment.

Third Degree Reiki

The third and highest degree of reiki is sometimes called the Master Degree. One who has passed into this degree has himself acquired the ability to pass on to others the reiki attunements. The secret way to do this is revealed during the attunement to the master degree. The student receives the final and most powerful symbol and the ability to use it, and is certified as a reiki teacher.

How Reiki Works

While reiki has different effects on each recipient and the results are extremely individualized due to a number of factors, it can be said that reiki caused five main effects. These are:

Reiki calms the mind and body.

Recipients of reiki feel a profound release and a sensation of calmness come over their physical and mental faculties. Then practitioners of other healing arts such as reflexology or massage receive reiki attunement, their ability to affect this calming sensation is enabled and enhanced. When a person suffers, he is out of balance. Reiki brings back essential balance to all systems of the mind and body. Mood swings and emotional outbursts are lessoned, causing much less burden on the person's vital energies. When the mind and body are calm they are far more receptive to joy and happiness, and less likely to become stuck in negative thoughts and beliefs, which cause negative behavior patters. By becoming calm and balanced a person can experience a greatly improved outlook on life. Reiki induces a feeling of deep relaxation often like nothing the recipient has felt before.

Reiki opens energy blockages.

As we will see in the next section, the body holds energy in several "centers" through which there must be constant flow of energy for well-being to be experiences. Reiki facilitates the free flow of energy through these centers.

Reiki releases tension and pressure.

Once the aforementioned blockages have been removed, reiki can begin to remove pockets of tension within the body. As the tension is unwound and released, the person experiences a balanced flow of energy which allows a harmonious, healthful lifestyle. The body is now ready to be detoxified and rid itself of dangerous buildups of unhealthy physical and mental pollution. Stress is such a ubiquitous problem in our modern society we scarcely notice its detrimental effects, thinking them part of "normal" existence. In fact, the affects of stress and tension are quite harmful and the body is called upon to exercise its defensive mechanisms to counteract them almost continuously. This exhausts the energies and causes any number of undesirable outcomes in the person's life and health. The ability to release built-up tension from environmental and societal factors and to protect against their affects is vital to a harmonious and fulfilling existence. Reiki can affect this change.

Reiki transmits healing energy.

Once the body has been purified the recipient is ready to receive healing energies. The transmission of the universal healing energies takes place in exact balance with the needs of the recipient and his ability to receive and use the energies. New vitality is pulsed from the practitioner to the recipient.

Reiki reinforces the body's own healing powers.

Reiki reinforces the person's own vital powers by raising his ability to use his innate energies and by strengthening his aura. The cure then essentially takes place from within the recipients own entity. Once the blocked areas are cleared up, energy is available to the person to deal with his life in a more constructive way, rather than wasting energy in holding onto the blocked places. The life force begins to flow and all organs of the body are strengthened and rejuvenated, allowing health, which is the body's nature state, to reinstate itself. If the person suffers acutely from a particular disease or condition, reiki allows the mind to let in the understanding of why that condition manifested. This understanding leads to profound release, and the need to suffer that particular ailment vanishes. Reiki works on all levels – spiritual, emotional, and physical, to bring about full healing. The reiki treatment raises the vibrational tenor of the entire body.

How Reiki is performed

Unlike many healing arts, reiki can be administered anywhere, anytime, and under most conditions. The recipient, as we have said, need not even be physically present. There are certain conditions which would be optimum however, and which the practitioner would do well so seek before beginning to deliver a treatment. An environment where the air is as unpolluted as possible (a smoky room would not be advised), and where a minimum level of calm and quiet it present will help one concentrate and allow the energy to flow. Most reiki healers prefer low lighting such as that provided by a candle or too, and perhaps some gentle music in the background. This puts both healer and recipient into receptive moods and the serenity will enhance their enjoyment of the process. Fragrant oils can be used to scent the air, giving an atmosphere of upliftment. Jasmine and lavender are relaxing choices. A room which is used frequently for treatment should be energy-cleared between recipients. The healer can choose from any number of effective ways to clear the energies of the previous interaction and to freshen the environment. Burning incense, airing the room, ringing a bell with a pleasing frequency in all corners of the room, are all possible ways to get the healing space ready for the next person.

The recipient can receive reiki either sitting or reclining (or even standing) but in order to assure maximum relaxation, the reclining or lying down position is usually preferred. Raising the lower legs to flatten the spine can allow for the most comfort for most people. The arms and legs should never be crossed over the body as this will block the vital flow of energies. Likewise the practitioner himself must keep his limbs open and uncrossed at any point. Even when reiki is administered in a public or crowded place, the rule against crossing limbs must be strictly adhered to.

The recipient should remove all metal ornaments worn on his person such as belt buckles, watches, and the like. Metal objects which encircle a part of the body can cut off the flow of vital energy. Jewelry should also be removed as the stones and crystals it contains affect the body's energy frequencies.

Reiki is delivered from the top of the body, downward. When the entire body is not involved in the treatment, it is started from the uppermost point of the area to be treated. The practitioner closes the fingers on both hands and slightly cups his hands. He then gently puts his hands on the recipient's body, applying just the slightest amount of pressure. Both hands are used, one next to the other. When paired parts of the body are treated (such as the knees), one hand is placed on each part.

Reiki can also be delivered without touch, even when performed in close proximity to the recipient. Some people are reluctant to be touched by the healer for religious reasons or simply reasons of modesty. In these cases the hands can be placed five to seven inches above the body and no effectiveness will be lost.

Once the reiki treatment has begun, the healer must be vigilant never to break away from the process or "let go". When moving the hands along the recipient's body, the practitioner maintains constant and continuous contact, slowly moving down, placing one hand against the other as he descends. The practitioner's energy should never leave the aura of the recipient until the end of the treatment. If the recipient must change position (such as from back to stomach), the healer's hand remains poised within his energy as he does so.

A full body reiki treatment will always begin at the head. The healer calls upon his guides and helpers who reside in the spirit realm and taps into their energy. He may call forth a vision of the great reiki masters or of the practitioner from whom he received attunement. This is done in the traditional prayer stance, palms together, and eyes closed, for a few seconds or a minute. Once linked to the great reiki chain, the healer is ready to begin.

Standing at the side of the head, the healer places his palms gently over the recipient's eyes. While holding the hands over the eyes, the practitioner is able to gauge the energy flow of the recipient. He maintains this position for several moments until he feels the places in the recipient's body which need the reiki the most. The recipient "draws out" the energy from the practitioner in just the amount needed to affect a healing. The healer moves his palms slowly to each of these places in turn, remaining in each until the energy is "returned" to his hands, telling him that the recipient has filled himself to the maximal amount of energy needed in that area. The recipient's subconscious makes a "decision" as to how much of the vital energy to allow in during a session. A very sensitive reiki practitioner knows exactly when it is time to move on to another part of the body. Usually three to five minutes is the optimal treatment time for each area or organ of the body, but this varies according to the individual.

When the reiki has been delivered to the head, ears, temples, clavicle, and lower rib regions (with the addition at times of the groin area, knees, and feet), the recipient is asked to turn over onto his stomach in order to receive reiki to the shoulders and lower back.

When treatment is finished, the healer removes his hands from the recipient's body with a slow, gentle movement, never a sudden or sharp one.

Chakras

During the treatment, the body's *energy centers* are cleared and balanced, allowing the vital life force to flow freely. Let's take a look at these centers, which are called *chakras*.

The human body has seven "energy centers". Each of these centers regulates the flow of energy controlling particular physical and emotional processes. The energy must flow through the centers in a balanced and unhindered way in order for us to experience well-being. Each chakra serves as a nerve center for a particular area of a person's awareness and experience. The energies of each chakra emit along a certain frequency which controls the various systems on the spiritual, emotional, and physical planes. They correspond with the glands and organs of the body, as well as to particular colors and perceptions. When you picture the body as taking up the space of a sphere, and cross-sections are cut from the sphere in a horizontal manner, each chakra is one cross-sectional ring, including the body itself and the surrounding area, sometimes called the aura. While we will speak of each energy center individually, it is essential to understand that all of the energies of the body are interconnected and work in tandem with one another. When there is blockage or imbalance in one area, the same can usually be found in another. Complete opening and balancing of all of the centers is therefore ideal. Each chakra energizes a particular gland of the endocrine system. When the delicate endocrine or hormonal system is in sync, the body experiences well being and glowing health. When the chakras experience blockage, the corresponding hormone is affected and can set off a chain of imbalances within the body having profound negative effects. Reiki brings this system back into essential balance.

1. The Base Chakra.

The base, or root chakra is located in the anal-genital area. Our powerful instinct for survival and our sense of security and power all reside in this energy center. Passion, strength, and vitality are controlled here. The reproductive system, excretory system, and intestines are associated with the base chakra. Our perceptions of ourselves in relation to the material world are controlled by its energies. Our feeling of stability and security, and our belief in our ability to survive are based here as well. The base chakra drives our need for sexual activity as a way of ensuring continuation of physical life. Self-defense and the willingness to fight for one's preservation as well as the motivation to work to provide sustenance, originate in the root energy center. It allows us to ascertain danger and prevents us from fool-hardy risks. The will to live, without which there is nothing else, is based here. When the root chakra is closed or out of balance, we might feel ungrounded, as if we've lost our connection to mother earth. Our stability and balance will seem fragile, and we may develop an unhealthy relationship to the material aspects of physical life. Someone whose base chakra is blocked might also become a risk taker, or be beset with physical ills such as constipation, fatigue, lack of energy, and bone and tissue disorders. In addition to reiki treatment, and in conjunction with it, the following crystals align the energies of the base chakra: Jet, smoky quartz, garnet, onyx, hematite, red jasper, bloodstone, and ruby. The healthy functioning of the thymus gland is connected to the base chakra. The color associated with this chakra is deep red.

2. The Sex Chakra.

The second chakra, moving up from the base, is the sex chakra, located in the pelvic area. This chakra controls the sex drive and sexual activity. Of vital importance both to reiki and the Tantra, the energies here are extremely powerful and affect all other systems of the body and mind. The musculature, the sex organs and fertility are linked to the second energy center. The testicles, ovaries, and prostrate, as well as the lymphatic system of the body are balanced by the sex chakra. Creativity, self-actualization and the finding of ones true vocation are based here. The energies of the sex chakra must be activated in order for us to take action to realize our desires and to express our talents and potentials. Honesty is based here as well. The ability to be open and forthright arises from the movement of sexual energy through the second chakra. A person's sense of uniqueness and his individuality are also driven by sex chakra energies. Blockages or closure of the sex chakra can cause breakdown in function of the kidneys, bladder, and digestive system. Imbalance here can cause an unhealthy attitude toward or even fear of sex. Impotence, lack of passion, and weak sexual impulses may result, while in some people the imbalance manifests a preoccupation or obsession with sex. Obsessive behavior resulting from energy imbalance cannot, however, provide pleasure. Allergies and muscle cramps are also afflictions caused by an imbalance in this area. When the sex chakra is in perfect balance, however, it leads to a confident sense of self and ability to flourish mentally and emotionally. Our ability to empathize and feel at one with others, allowing us to see others as part of us, while at the same time separate, requires a balancing of the sex chakra energy. This ability is vital, as we will see, to the practice of Tantric sex. A closed or imbalanced sex chakra will effectively close the door on possible enriching relationships both sexual and otherwise. An ability to open up to another without fear and with total abandon relies on a complete balancing of the energies here. The color orange represents the sex chakra and fosters the balancing of its energies. Crystals and stones: Moonstone, fire opal, citrine, and topaz.

3. The Solar Plexus Chakra.

The third chakra is located from the sternum to just above the naval. It is the center of personal strength, vitality, and ambition. The energies of this chakra are ideally developed between the ages of eight and twelve and make up our feeling of inner strength and the stability of our character. The diaphragm, the digestive system, the liver, the spleen and the pancreas are all associated with this chakra, as well as the respiratory system and the sympathetic nervous system. A person's ability to relate to others and to affect his surroundings in a positive manner is rooted here. The ego, self-realization, and our ability to connect to the world around us are driven by the energies of this center. Awareness of personal likes and preferences and the ability to be in touch with and understand our own emotions lie here as well. This chakra's energies allow us our place in society or in any group and our desire to seek status or power and achievement. Logic, rationality, and general intelligence also lie here. The individuation or our personality and character stem from the third chakra, and the extent to which this is accomplished defines our uniqueness in the world. When energies are balanced here we are able to play out our role in life to the utmost, utilizing our special talents and abilities in order to achieve and to contribute. We feel abundant, joyful, and content. When the third chakra is blocked however, we feel stymied, as if we have not been able to find or follow our chosen path. We feel imbalanced and frustrated and as if we have not realized our true destiny. We may abuse others in an unbalanced effort to achieve status and power, and become unduly competitive, restless or ambitious. Balance of the third chakra is vital then for self-esteem, self-satisfaction, and a feeling of relaxation. Physical problems which can stem from a blockage of third chakra energies include digestive disorders, ulcers, heart disease, allergies, diabetes, and gallstones. The adrenal gland functions optimally when this chakra is balanced. Stones and crystals which can help in balancing the energies of the third chakra: peridot, topaz, amber, citrine, and tiger's eye. Yellow is the color of the third chakra.

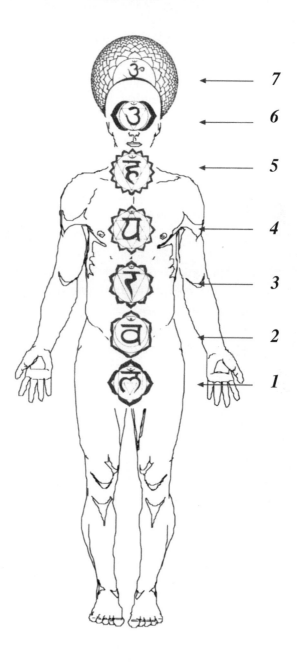

4. The Heart Chakra

Located in the middle of the body, in line with the heart, the fourth chakra is the chakra of love. The energy here represents harmony, affection, good will, and love. It is optimally developed fully between the ages of thirteen and fifteen. The lungs, back, skin, hands, circulatory system, and of course, the heart, are associated with this chakra. The heart chakra links the first three lower chakras, and when the heart chakra is out of balance, so are the others. Our ability to care, to give and receive devotion and love, and to truly open up to another are tied up in this chakra. Just as importantly, this chakra must be balanced in order to achieve self love, without which love for another will be compromised if not impossible. When the heart chakra energies are in balance we achieve self acceptance and a compassion for and understanding of ourselves. We release self-loathing, self-recrimination, and self-judgment. This opens up our ability to offer the same to another. Our physical and sexual encounters are infused with sensitivity and understanding only when the heart chakra is unblocked and energies flow through it unimpeded. As we will see later when discussing Tantric sex, an open heart chakra is absolutely necessary for optimum sexual and sensual experiences. We must be able to identify with and feel deep empathy with our partner, and this can only be achieved through the peeling away of layers of personal armor or self-protective behaviors. Openness to ourselves is vital before we can open to a partner. Also based in this energy center is the essential ability to forgive. Forgiveness is a vital part of our opening to another being and to our innermost selves. When the heart chakra is in open, we are able to give, but also to receive a like portion, leaving us in delightful and energizing balance. We will not cover up our feelings out of embarrassment, nor be reticent to provide what another needs for fear of being "taken". We are ready for a free and honest flow, and for complete harmony. A person with severe and complete blockage of the fourth chakra may appear cold, aloof, tense, and alienated. He may be perceived as bad or evil by those around him. Often a closed heart chakra is expresses in hostility, jealousy, or stinginess. The physical ailments such a blockage might foster include: heart disease and heart attacks, high blood pressure, fatigue, insomnia, and breathing difficulties. The thymus gland may malfunction when the heart chakra is closed. Crystals that can help in the opening and balancing of the heart chakra are: Rose quartz, aventurine, malachite, emerald, and jade. The colors pink and green carry the energies of this chakra.

5. The Throat Chakra

Located in the neck area, the fifth chakra contains the energies of communication. The ability to connect with our surroundings and interact with them in a meaningful way by expressing ourselves is linked to this chakra. When we think a thought, or have an opinion or reaction, our free-flowing ability to talk about or to otherwise communicate these is essential to our well-being and self image. A blocked throat chakra caused a build-up of unspoken thoughts and desires, a frustration of creative urges, and conflict between the observed and the acted upon. Expression of the inner world in the outer world is one of a human being's basic needs, and when our opportunity or ability to express is blocked, the results are dangerous indeed. Between the ages of fifteen and twenty one is the ideal span of time for development of communication talents. Open communication with and acceptance of self is just as important as communication with others. We must not block our truths from our conscious mind, lest we fall into "denial", which is essentially a blockage of the fifth chakra. All emotions, though perhaps felt through other energies, are given expression through the fifth chakra. Joy, love, happiness, and elation, as well as sadness, frustration, sadness, and grief, must be expressed and let out each in its time. The throat chakra is linked powerfully to the sex chakra, which controls creativity. When the throat chakra is open and balanced, creativity can flow, giving expression to our deepest emotions and desires. If we are out of communication with ourselves, we can't discern out own feelings, much less understand them. Thus creativity will be blocked. As important as being expressive, of course, is the ability to connect to the expressions coming forth from others. Communication is not one-sided, and the knack for being a good listener and for being sympathetic and empathetic is what makes for shared messages between people. When the fifth chakra is blocked, we cut ourselves off form the communications efforts of others, as well as from our ability to communicate with them. The throat chakra is also the center of honesty and integrity. Only when one is completely honest will his communications flow forth unimpeded. Lying and cheating will choke off the energies and close the chakra and cause distorted messages to emanate to ourselves and others. An open throat chakra will foster self-esteem, confidence, and openness. It will allow what is inside to flow forth naturally and joyfully, making its mark on our world. It fosters easy speech patterns and language usage. The person with an open throat chakra is aware of his feelings and their ebb and flow, giving them voice when appropriate and never denying them. A blocked throat chakra, on the other hand, can result in speech impediments, self-criticism, confusion, and lack of confidence. Not surprisingly, physical ailments caused by a blocked fifth chakra include those that afflict the ears, throat, vocal chords and neck. The functioning of thyroid gland is linked to the balance or imbalance of the throat chakra. The color associated with the throat chakra is blue. Crystals having frequencies helpful to the balancing of this chakra: Sodalite, blue lace agate, lapis lazuli, blue tourmaline, aquamarine, sapphire, and other blue stones.

6. The Third Eye Chakra

The middle of the forehead, above and between the eyes, is the location of the sixth chakra. Called the third eye because it opens up new ways of "seeing" not part of our normal sense of sight. The third eye is our window to intuition, imagination and connection with our higher beings. Our unconscious thoughts become available to our conscious minds through the energies of the sixth chakra. The brain receives its energies through the third eye chakra. Mental abilities, memory, and knowledge are balanced here. When the third eye chakra is open we are tuned in to our innate ability to receive messages from beyond conscious awareness. Non-verbal and non-physical become understandable and accessible. An open third eye allows harmony with oneness with the universe. The soul consists of elements not tied to the physical, and only through the opening and balancing of the sixth chakra can we get in touch with all aspects of the soul and feel entirely whole and at peace. The sixth chakra controls the nervous system, which in turn oversees the harmonious functioning of all that the brain controls from its command 'on high'. Telepathy and other extra-sensory perceptions are available to one whose third eye is open and balanced. When this chakra is blocked, as it often is in modern humanity, the intellect and reasoning powers of the person come to the fore and block out the all-important intuition. Logic takes over and pushes aside the channels to higher knowledge and understanding. In order to be open to the spiritual world or to spiritual teachings, an open third eye is essential. A balance between the spiritual and the rational, the conscious and the subconscious is fostered when this center is open. Furthermore, when the third eye is open, the brain itself comes into balance, causing the left and right hemispheres to function in harmony. Learning problems, depression, headaches, hearing and vision problems and mental exhaustion are all symptoms of a blocked sixth chakra. The pituitary gland depends on the balanced energy from the sixth chakra. The colors associated with the third eye chakra are violet and indigo blue.

Crystals often used to open the third eye are fluorite, lapidolite, sugelite, amethyst, and azurite.

7. The Crown Chakra

As its name implies, the crown chakra is located at the very top and center of the head. From this chakra we link with the All That Is, or universal enlightenment. Divine knowledge can only filter into our awareness if the crown chakra is open and balanced. The chakra of wisdom and unity, this is the energy center which opens us up to true spiritual illumination. By uniting the energies of all of the other chakras combined, the crown chakra raises us up to the highest frequency possible, allowing us to join with the cosmic energy system. With regard to sexual union, when the crown chakra is open, sex has the possibility of becoming blissful and mystical to the extreme. While the third eye opens up the possibility of reception of cosmic insight, if the crown chakra is blocked our awareness cannot integrate this insight. The energies of the crown chakra do not run our thoughts, but exist on a plane above thought, where understanding is instantaneous and effortless. All knowledge that exists is available to us when our seventh chakra is wide open and receiving. We are not separate from All That Is, but a part and particle of the entire universe. Opening the crown chakra helps the other chakras release their blockages as well. When the crown is open we receive understanding of what is holding the other centers closed, and the release manifests as a result of this understanding. Meditation sometimes affords an opening of the crown chakra, allowing in cosmic energies and influencing the person both consciously and unconsciously. The differences between the physical and non-physical become blurred, as do the differences between internal and external being. When habitual opening of the crown chakra is achieved, it fosters a calm feeling of oneness with the universe and balance and harmony with the self. Complete and utter self understanding and self acceptance results from a crown chakra that is totally opened and unblocked. Actions flow as a result of complete "knowing" which is different from "planning". An understanding of time as an illusion and the present existence as being part of a continuum where past, present and future are all happening simultaneously is integrated. Life becomes a dance of joy and harmony, and emotions no longer involuntarily drive the person's actions. He is in control, effortlessly and joyously. He is part of the celestial realms while existing in physical body. He truly knows the "best of both worlds". When the crown chakra is blocked or closed, however, the person feels he is an entity separate from the rest of the universe. He does not feel his connection with All That Is, and may even be confused, angry and frustrated at times, and full of questions as to the meaning of life and he part in creation. Boredom and feelings of lack are the domain of those with blocked crown chakras, as is fear of death. A person who blames others for the circumstances of his life is out of touch with his connection to source energy, and can see himself as separate, outside the flow, a victim. The colors associated with the seventh chakra are white, gold, silver, and purple. It is symbolized by the shape of a lotus flower with a thousand petals.

The crystals that can be used to help open this chakra are diamonds, clear quartz, selenite, pyrite, and angelite.

A full body reiki treatment will bring all of the chakras into balance. When the practitioner wishes to balance one in particular, or to perform a shorter treatment designed specifically for balancing the chakras, he places one hand in front of and in back of the area of each chakra in turn, holding the hands a few inches from the body. He holds his hands in this position, flowing energy to the chakra, for several minutes or more, depending on the need of the recipient. When either of these treatments is complete, the recipient's chakras will be open and his endocrine glands will being to function normally.

The Tantra

Many people have heard the term "Tantra" or "Tantric Sex", and believe them to mean a form of intense and uninhibited sexual intercourse. Some are vaguely aware that Tantric sex originated "long ago and far away" and that it somehow ties in with ancient religious practice. Interestingly, however, the word Tantra, which originates from the Sanskrit, does not mean sex at all, but rather "written doctrine", or "authoritative way". The word Tantra can also mean scientific treatise, formula, strategy, doctrine, theory or rule. Other definitions include extension, expansion" and manifestation. Some scholars have attributed the origins of the word to a combination of the Sanskrit words "tanot" and "tryat", meaning the opening up and liberation of the conscious mind.

The ancient Tantric teachings are thought to have originated with a divine revelation which was put into written form. The Tantric writings include many fascinating secrets and instructions on a full range of spiritual and practical subjects. Tantra teaches the connection between the physical and spiritual dimensions and points the way to a harmonious existence on both planes.

In ancient India, the Tantra was studied as a path to enlightenment and fulfillment of human potential. The best known of the Tantric texts, the Kama Sutra, was written in India in the seventeenth century. The Tantra is far older than this, however. As long ago as seventeen thousand years before the Common Era, Tantric symbols were inscribed on the walls of caves. Tantra spread over the centuries throughout the Far East and even to Egypt and Greece. Tantra has been embraced by followers of many of the world's religions. Tantric Buddhists, Tantric Hindus and Tantric Taoists all extracted from the Tantric teachings that which they believed could help them on the path to enlightenment.

Indeed, the most compelling of the Tantric teachings are those which prescribe techniques leading to sexual fulfillment beyond the ordinary. Sex, according to the Tantras, must be undertaken with an openness and abandon. Tantric sex transcends ordinary consciousness and connects the individual or couple with spirit. The Tantra explains how we can use our body and its energies to lift our existence beyond the limits of the five bodily senses and rise to a cosmic level. Time and place become non-existent as we achieve the ultimate experience.

Tantric Sex

As we said in our discussion of reiki, all of the body's functions rely on the free and uninhibited flow of energy. This certainly includes the sexual functions and the organs associated with sexual activity. "Sexual energy" is a term we sometimes use, perhaps not fully understanding that it is the same essential energy that drives every activity. The energy becomes sexual when we consciously direct it toward achievement of sexual pleasure. By focusing the energy which flows through us at all times toward the sex organs and by assuring that the energy reaches them in the fullest manner, we increase sexual pleasure a hundred fold.

The sex organs are powerful movers and receivers of energy. They exist in a fragile balance however, and can malfunction or even cease to function if the chakras are not open and allowing energy to pulse through them. Sometimes the sex organs seem to be performing their tasks, but do so in a perfunctory manner which brings little satisfaction. A person who is able to perform the sex act, but is unaware that his chakras are closed is missing a huge portion of the potential that is within him. An awareness of how the flow of energy affects the joy we receive from sex can open up endless possibilities for change in this area. When sex is truly spiritual, fulfilling, and joyful, it can transform lives.

Modern physicians often claim that sexual activity is healthy and necessary for a balanced life. Mental health practitioners sometimes prescribe sexual activity as a way to relieve stress. Here, we focus on the use of sex to uplift a couple practicing together to the heights of joy and spiritual fulfillment.

The Tantric teachings assume a two person alliance for the purpose of experiencing Tantric sex. A loving, caring relationship is a prerequisite for Tantric sex to achieve its potential for the participants. At the same time, practicing Tantric sex can move an already good relationship into spheres of intimacy and perfection not even imagined beforehand.

The Tantra takes into account the existence of both masculine and feminine components in the man and woman alike. Unless each partner is willing to accept all aspects of himself as perfect and desirable, the sex will be out of balance. Total self acceptance is vital. Therefore, the man must allow himself to be soft and vulnerable at times, while the woman must be willing to show her aggressive will and her strength. Most of us are familiar with the Tao concepts of Yin and Yang. Yin and Yang symbolize, simultaneously, earth and heaven, male and female, light and dark. These aspects are present in our sexual make-ups, with one or the other being dominant depending on our gender. As a sexual encounter takes place, yin and yang energy are exchanged back and forth, until the union comes into perfect balance and symmetry.

Tantric sex is the correct use of the body's sexual energy. When done right, the sexual act can arouse the Kundalini energy – a concentrated store of energy based in the lower spine, at the base chakra. The Kundalini is like a curled up snake, lying dormant, but ready to unwind and use its intensely powerful energy for good or for ill. The Kundalini is usually symbolized by the image of a sleeping serpent, coiled three times, with its tail in its mouth. When it is awakened, its power can cause an amazingly effective healing and cleansing experience.

How to Have Tantric Sex

The Tantras teach that in order to have successful sex with a partner, we must first be able to "succeed" at solo sex. A deep understanding is needed of our own sexual nature and of what arouses us and brings us satisfaction. We must know how our bodies respond to different types of stimulation and be intimately in touch with our body's secrets. The Tantric teachings stress the importance of this self-exploration and self-knowledge and their vital role in the outcome of a sexual partnership. Reiki can be used as a tool to energize the sexual areas and to balance and relax us before self-stimulation.

According to the Tantras, nothing at all is forbidden, nothing is off limits. Complete freedom to try and enjoy anything at all is essential. An attitude of anything goes and a feeling of open possibilities is the lesson of Tantric sex.

Tantric sex is not meant to be spontaneous sex, nor is it appropriate for a "quickie". Preparation of mind, body, and environment are essential for the success of the encounter. Tantric sex is far more about what precedes and energizes sexual intercourse than it is about the culminating act itself.

Before beginning, it is important to bring the body into balance by using reiki or another system of balancing all of the chakras. If there is blockage in any area, the sex and base chakras will be affected, and the Tantric sex will not have its greatest potential.

Preparing the environment

Once the partners have been brought into energy balance, they can turn to the room they have chosen and begin to bring it too into positive energy. Choose a place which has not absorbed the energy of arguments or sadness. If this is not possible, the negative energies in the space can be cleared using a number of space clearing techniques. If the space is highly compromised and feels uncomfortably negatively charged, it is advisable to clear it the day before attempting Tantric sex.

Place coarse salt around the perimeter of the room and light candles in the four corners. Allow several hours for the energies to be purified. Discard the salt, and thoroughly clean the room. Another technique to dissipate negative energy is bell-ringing. Find a bell with a pleasing resonance to you, and walk slowly around the perimeter of the room, ringing the bell, stopping to ring longer in places where the energies feel resistant or thick. Clapping loudly will work if you can't find a bell, and doing both clapping and bell-ringing, one after the other, is even better. After energetically clearing the space, it is helpful to consecrate it in your mind by stating your intention to come together with a partner in a positive way in this space, and to create only joy and perfect union within these walls.

A clean and fresh body is as important as the cleanliness of the environment. Washing one another, especially, when accompanied by positive intent and a bit of ritual, can greatly enhance the experience of Tantric sex. Washing one another is a very intimate activity, and when one is washed by a partner, intense sexual feelings can be aroused.

Along with your partner, discuss the atmosphere that is most desirable during sex. Lighting, either electric or candle, should be low, and not harsh or bright. When using candles, be sure they are sturdy and long burning so as not to require tending during lovemaking. Music can be a welcome addition to the atmosphere, and the partners should decide together on a pleasing, soothing selection. The music can be stimulating, and if the couple wishes to dance a little before sex, all the better, as dancing is a marvelous prelude to what is to come.

The sense of smell should not be forgotten when preparing the space for a romantic encounter. An inexpensive oil burner can be used to infuse the room with a scent pleasing to both partners. Choose a good quality pure aromatic oil, or mixture of two or more.

After bathing, it is a good idea to don some garments which have been well planned beforehand. The Tantras do not preach nudity for sex, but on the contrary, they understand the potential of certain articles of clothing to arouse sexual desire. Covering the body, at least partially, can be provocative and erotic. The same is true of makeup and jewelry. Adorning the body rather than simply presenting it in its raw nakedness is considered by the Tantric masters to be part of the sexual dance. Experiment with the feel of different fabrics and textures, each of which has its own erotic nature. Color too, can make the body more interesting and sensual. Silk, satin, and even fur are some examples that might be considered.

Once the preparations and purifications have taken place,

it's time to take stock again of the state of our energy. As mentioned, balance is vital. In addition, we should achieve a state of relaxation before attempting a Tantric sexual encounter. This is not to say we can't be sexually aroused, but the arousal must be strictly toward our partner in a positive sense, as opposed to the arousal induced by anger, frustration, or stress. Reiki can be used to induce a positive state of deep relaxation, causing the oxygen uptake of the blood to maximize, giving a feeling of well-being and vitality.

Meditation can be useful as a relaxation tool, allowing us to let go of recurring stressful thoughts and enter a state where we are in touch with our own energies and true natures. According to the Tantras, meditation is one of the most important preludes to excellent sex. When we are in contact with our higher selves, or our inner beings, we are then able to open up truer contact with another soul. We are available in a far more intimate manner to our partner when we have gotten in touch with our own essence. There can be no barriers, no defenses, when we are completely relaxed and allowing our true natures to come to the fore.

Be sure to set aside enough time for Tantric sex. When there are time constraints the partners feel rushed and this can lead to stress. This cannot be emphasized too much. Attempt the experience only when time is unlimited and distractions or interruptions unlikely.

Let's Begin

Once you and your partner have purified your bodies and the space you will use for Tantric sex, you have set the stage with fragrance and lighting, adorned yourselves with clothing and ornaments, and relaxed and meditated until you have reached a sublime state of readiness..... It's time to begin.

The period of "foreplay", or slow and deliberate arousal, should take a considerable amount of time and attention. For both partners, the length and quality of foreplay can determine the intensity of desire and the amount of pleasure inherent in the final release. At least twenty minutes of foreplay is desirable, and more will only enhance the response.

Tantra preaches arousal of the entire body, not just the traditional erogenous zones. It's best to leave the obvious areas for last, while slowly arousing the rest of the body using caresses, kisses, or any other form of slow gentle contact. The man especially, should have his penis and scrotum left for last, while the woman attends lovingly to the rest of his anatomy. Allow desire to build up slowly, as you pay attention to one another in a caring and affectionate matter.

Deep kissing is an important element of foreplay. Take time to taste one another, to explore one another's mouth and tongue, keeping the eyes open in order to express and to see one another's pleasure. According to the Tantras, the exchange of body fluids (including saliva) is vital to the connection between the partners. By taking in the fluids of another you show complete acceptance and love. The Tantrists even believed that a woman's saliva was a health elixir for a man, giving him strength and stamina, especially if he sucks her tongue at the moment of female orgasm!

Oral stimulation is very important to Tantric sex. The Tantras teach that by kissing, licking, or sucking, the sexual energies are multiplied and that these methods offer extreme pleasure to the passive partner, no matter to which body part they are applied. Mutual oral sex can be extremely effective, although it takes concentration to receive and give intense pleasure simultaneously.

Positions for intercourse

Of course, in most sexual encounters, the moment of penetration inevitably arrives. In Tantric sex that moment occurs when foreplay naturally melts into intercourse, as both partners are supremely aroused and ready. There are almost infinite positions that can be used for intercourse, but we'll mention those described by the Tantric treatises, since any others are variations on these basic themes.

Man on top partners facing one another:

This position is the most widely practiced, probably because of the possibility it affords for kissing and eye to eye contact, both of which increase intimacy and a feeling of connection between the partners. Indeed, the Tantras consider the eye's gaze to be very important, since it adds to the energy exchange during the sexual act. Men often prefer to be on top since this gives them the most control and offers them the freest movement. With the woman in the passive position the man can decide the rhythm and depth of penetration. Usually when the man is on top, the woman is on her back, legs spread. This is often referred to as the "missionary position". For variation, the woman can draw up her knees, or even close her legs around the man's back and torso. Another position, which requires concentration on the part of both partners, involves the woman straightening out her legs to enclose the penis between them, while the man keeps his legs outside hers.

Woman on top, partners facing one another:

Positions where the woman is on top can also afford kissing and eye contact. With this position, the woman takes control, deciding on the depth and rhythm of penetration that are optimum to her pleasure. Usually, the woman kneels with her knees to either side of the man. An even more intimate position has the man sitting cross-legged, while the woman straddles him from above.

Woman on top, woman facing man's feet.

With this position the woman has control, but no eye or lip contact, obviously is possible.

Back to front position.

When the man penetrates the woman from behind, the deepest vaginal penetration is allowed. This position can be struck lying down, standing, or kneeling. Side-lying, or "spooning" is perhaps the most common position for rear-entry.

Orgasm

As the moment of release approaches, both partners should be fully aware and in control. Breathing deeply and with awareness will enhance the response and each partner's awareness of the other's energies. According to the Tantras, the moment of orgasm is the union of spirits. It is the moment the physical moves to meet the spiritual plane. As the energy moves from the base chakra all the way up through the crown, the physical focus becomes non-physical.

The Tantras teach that male orgasm is less important than female! The male orgasm. when accompanied by ejaculation, weakens the man, while the woman can orgasm again and again with no loss of sexual energy taking place!

Tantric sex for the male consists of three stages: arousal, plateau, and orgasm. During the arousal stage, erection occurs and the man begins to feel desire. The plateau stage is the period of time the man maintains his desire as it escalates toward culmination. The orgasm usually takes place simultaneously with ejaculation and constitutes the peak, and then the release, of desire.

The Tantras teach that male orgasm can occur with or without ejaculation, and that the two needn't be synonymous of one another. They also teach that a man, like a woman, should be able to enjoy numerous orgasms with no recovery time needed, provided, of course, that ejaculation has not taken place. As long as the life energy is not wasted through the shedding of the semen, the man can remain able to experience numerous orgasms. These "dry orgasms" are unlimited, and were believed by the Tantrists to be desirable for a man's physical and emotional health.

Furthermore, when semen is not ejaculated, the male orgasm does not deplete the man, and leaves him as vital and awake as before the orgasm! The usual phenomenon of the man rolling over and falling asleep directly after sex will not occur when orgasm without ejaculation has taken place.

Male climax without ejaculation:

The concept that ejaculation is voluntary and under conscious control is a new one to most Western men, and the most important concept for a man to understand who undertakes Tantric sex.

36 TANTRIC SEX positions for intercourse

36 TANTRIC SEX positions for intercourse

Kundalini

The name *kundalini* is derived from the word *kunda*, which means space or aperture, and refers to the concave hollow that contains the human brain in the form of a curled-up snake. In men, the dormant kundalini is found in the perineum (the area between the scrotum and the anus). In women, it resides at the base of the uterus, in the cervix. The kundalini is described as a snake that is curled up three and a half times and closes the opening of the *sushumna* nerve in the center of the spine with its mouth.

This energy has been given different names in different cultures, and the oldest documentation of it by the name *kundalini* was discovered amongst the Indians.

There are two types of kundalini energy: potential and kinetic. In its potential form, the kundalini represents *shakti* or dormant power, while in its kinetic form, it is realized as a female divinity. Once aroused, but not yet under control, it is represented by the angry woman, the goddess Kali, who is naked, dark, and wears a necklace of 108 human skulls that represent previous lives. Kali's extended blood-red tongue symbolizes *rajo guna,* the symbol of creative energy, and urges the practitioner to take control of his *rajo guna.*

Every person has a special form of energy, which is dormant in most of us, develops slowly in some, and is completely aroused in a few. This energy has neither shape nor dimensions, but it has infinite abilities.

"Useful" awareness is represented by the snake in many faiths and traditions. Its three loops represent the three parts of Om (or Aum): past, present and future; the three *goons* (attributes): *tamas* (inertia), *rajas* (creative activity) and *satva* (purified form); the three states of consciousness: wakefulness, sleep and dreaming; and the three types of experience: subjective, sensory and a lack of experience. The half loop responds to the "point" in the Om and represents a state of lofty and elevated consciousness that goes beyond wakefulness, sleep and dreaming.

When the kundalini is aroused correctly and is under control, it is represented by the female divinity *Durga*, who appears as a higher, more refined and generous form of the subconscious. Now the practitioner can make use of it and amass power with its help. The beautiful goddess Durga sits astride a tiger. She has eight arms, which represent the eight elements of the human being. She wears a necklace of 52 human heads, which represent her wisdom and power. These heads represent the 52 letters of the Sanskrit alphabet as well as the external embodiment of the "unrevealed holy sound" that the Indians call *Naad*. This is "the word" of the Christians, the "saying" of the Jews ("And God said, Let there be light, and there was light"), the *"qalma i-ilhi"* of the Moslems, the music of the spheres of the Pythagoreans, and so on. *Durga* is a superconscious form of kundalini. She symbolizes the burning of the cumulative karma from previous lifetimes. The center of the root, *Muladhara*, is aroused, eliminates bad influences that have accumulated during the course of life, and grants tranquillity and strength.

The aroused Kundalini passes through the seven energy centers or chakras. The lowest chakra, which is located below the base of the spine, is called *Muladhara*, and the highest, which is found at the top of the head, is called *Sahasrara*. When a person reaches the highest energy center, he attains a higher level of awareness, experiences it, and finally lives in it.

This book defines what kundalini is and discusses different methods for arousing it and ways of identifying and recognizing it, as well as the insights that stem from this arousal.

Kundalini yoga is one of the yoga methods that combines several types of yoga: *Hatha, Tantra, Mantra, Laya* and *Raja*. The objective of this yoga method is to arouse the "dormant energy" at the base of the spine, which is called kundalini in the East and is better known to most of us as "spiritual life force."

In the quest for a common denominator among the different traditions, it transpired that it lies in the perennial (eternal) philosophy that represents the metaphysical system of the prophets, saints and sages in all religions and traditions.

Human beings can be religious or secular Jews, Christians, Moslems, Hindus, Buddhists or conscious atheists, and there will still be full consensus among them. Evidently, kundalini is the root of the enlightened person, no matter what his faith or tradition may be. In other words, the kundalini belongs to all the faiths and all the religions in the world.

A systematic presentation of this philosophy is offered in the *Bhagvadghita*, a Hindu poem that forms a part of the *Mahabarata* epos that merges several philosophical theories of Hinduism and accommodates them.

The *Vedas,* the principal Hindu sacred writings, described three paths for seeking the "truth":

1. Behakti yoga, or the path of devotion, for those whose hearts are more developed than their minds;

2. Jenana yoga, or the path of knowledge, for those whose minds are more developed than their hearts;

3. Karma yoga, for those in whom a balance exists between the heart and the mind (the intellect).

Hundreds of years ago, the guru *Gorak Nat* and others invented *Hatha yoga* for those whose minds and hearts were not sufficiently developed to lead to the arousal of the kundalini.

Kundalini yoga is in fact a combination of all of the approaches: it is built according to a systematic and qualitative criterion of development and is considered to be the shortest path to God. This book briefly surveys this tradition and also mentions details that are suitable for people who have only a limited amount of time for in-depth reading, but nevertheless want to become acquainted with the topic in a fulfilling manner.

What is the factor that is responsible for the differences between people? What differentiates between a person who achieves (sometimes with only a slight effort) and a person who fails in his endeavors (despite an enormous effort)? The answer is kundalini. Almost all of the faiths and traditions speak about this energy, even though the names for it and the definitions of it differ from one tradition to the next.

In this book, we will progress from the general to the specific, from theory to practice. We will begin with the energetic bodies and the chakras and conclude with practical exercises.

Preparatory exercises

This course of preparatory exercises is necessary for increasing the body's capability and also for receiving ki and channeling it. It is a preparation for the suitable practice that we are about to discuss. It links the meridian of conception and the governor meridian and creates a whole energy circuit in the body. This is performed by focusing the energy inward or by meditating.

1

Direct your awareness at your hara or navel. After some time, you will feel warmth that attests to the building up of ki.

Transfer your awareness to the root chakra or *hoi-yin*, and then upward toward the spine. Stop for a moment at the *ming-man* point (at the height of the kidneys), and then direct the ki upward to the crown chakra.

At this point, there is no need to make any effort; just permit a smooth flow of energy. Hold the energy in the crown chakra for about ten minutes, and then direct your awareness to Ajna (the third eye chakra).

Continue the downward flow of energy to your navel or hara region. Hold it there for some time until you feel warmth, and then start the cycle over again by moving it down to the root chakra.

Repeat the flow cycle a few times – as many as you can do comfortably – and gradually increase it to tens of rounds each time you sit down to perform it. Continue doing this until you become skilled at it. Then, continue the exercise for creating a link between the ground and your feet. Use your consciousness to move energy from your navel to the center of the root (*hoi-yin*).

Now divide the energy into two parts: send one downward, to behind your thigh, and from there to behind your knee.

Afterwards, direct the energy to your calves and feet.

2

On the feet, the chakras are located at *yung chuan* – acupuncture point K-1, known as *"bubbling spring"* – which joins the body electrically to the energy of the earth.

When your feet have warmed up sufficiently, move ki to your big toes and to your knees via the front of your legs. Remember that the energy must flow from the earth through your feet. The upward flow inside your thighs and back must continue to the *hoi-yin* or center of the root.

Now you must send the ki back up the spine, and at the point between your shoulder blades, you must divide it between your two arms. Transmit it inside your arms until it reaches the middle of your hands.

Pay attention to the feeling and make the current flow into your middle fingers and from there to the upper side of your arms.

When the current reaches your shoulders, it returns to the central current and to the crown via your spine and neck.

Go back to your hara via the central conduit. This grounding is the concluding part of the exercise, which collects the energy and prevents an electrical overload and discomfort. The hara is the starting and stopping place of energy.

Place your fist lightly above your navel region and rub it in lateral spiral movements of up to 6' (15 centimeters).

For a woman, the spiral must move about 40 times in a counter-clockwise direction, and afterwards about 20 times in a clockwise direction. The spiral movement is the opposite in a man, that is, about 40 times in a clockwise direction and about 20 times in a counter-clockwise direction.

The origin of the two important exercises that are common to Kundalini yoga and Chi-Kong that will be described below is apparently in India and Tibet, and from there they reached China and Japan. These exercises are very valuable for fortifying the health. Moreover, they have spiritual value.

Indians and Buddhists believe that the karma can be "reached" only in the human form, in the human body, and therein lies the importance of human birth. The mental entity that links the soul to the soul of God is also possible only in the form of the human universe.

Certain activities such as smoking, using drugs and drinking alcohol weaken the effect of Reiki. Therefore, Reiki must not be performed under the influence of these substances, since they neutralize the sanctity of the channel.

Kundalini exercise for women

Begin the microcosmic cycle while you are in a meditative state. Be aware of the ki as the energy of fire, raku, and move it from your navel (*hara*) to the root (*hoi-yin*), and then upward to your spine and to the center of the crown. Let the energy descend to the hara via the front of your body.

* Sit in the *sidha-yoni-asana* position, which is sitting on the floor with the heel of one foot pressing on Muladhara (the root chakra – against your vagina) and the heel of your other foot pressing against Svadhisthana (the second chakra – above your clitoris).

* Now apply *Mulbandha* – the root lock. Then place your tongue on your hard palate behind your teeth (*Khechri-mudra*). Sometimes, a small cushion can help you sit in this position. Now rub your two hands together in order to warm them.

* Massage your bare breasts with your warm hands, downward and upward. Make sure that your nipples are not aroused and repeat the action about 20 times.

* Feel the flow of *ki* in the root chakra (vagina), in the crown chakra and in the Ajna chakra (the third eye).

* An upward turn is called *dispersing*. Move the energy from your breasts, vagina, center of the crown and the Ajna chakra to the Anahata chakra (center of the heart), keeping your fingers on your nipples lightly.

* Repeat the set of about 20 massage cycles two to four times. Each time, make the ki move to the center of the heart.

* The direction of the turns must now be reversed. In other words, move downward and inward instead of upward and outward. These are *inverting* turns. The energy must be collected inside your nipples and moved to your spine behind your breasts.

* Repeat the set of 20 turns three to five times.

* Now move your hands from your breasts to the kidney point at the back of your body, behind your lowest ribs.

* Massage the region and gently shake it up to 20 times, and after a short rest, repeat the process three to five times. Be aware of the warmth in the kidney region.

* Afterwards, massage your lower abdomen, from your crotch to your ovaries, liver and gallbladder on the right side below your lowest ribs, and then the spleen on the left side.

* The outward and inward massage should be performed 40 times in each set.

* Afterwards, massage your vagina in order to store energy. Take a short break and pay attention to the spreading of the ki.

* Now place your right hand above your vagina and your left hand on the Anahata chakra. Be aware of the universal love that is created and draw it into your heart.

* Draw the energy of the earth inside, continue the microcosmic cycle, and conclude by storing energy inside the hara.

That is the end of the first exercise for women.

The result of these exercises is not just the opening of the nadis and the arousal of the kundalini, but also the conversion of sexual energy into spiritual force and universal love. Sexual energy gets lost during the woman's monthly cycle, ovulation and copulation.

Reiki exercises recycle this energy and turn it into ki for the production of serenity, inner happiness, physical health and the prevention of diseases. Moreover, the exercises balance hormonal cycles in the woman's body. Menopausal symptoms are likely to disappear with the dispersing turns, which result in "the turning back of the blood".

Dispersing turns tend to reduce the size of the chest, as opposed to inverting turns, which increase it. If you perform the two types of turns the same number of times, the hormones are balanced without changing the size of the chest. An extremely important occurrence is the renewed direction of the sexual ki toward the crown chakra, which is linked to menopause. However, a woman who wants to fall pregnant must reduce the number of turns to less than 100 per day. These exercises do not have any side effects such as delayed adolescence or heightened creativity and mental awareness.

Note: *The application of the root lock (Mulbandha) while sitting in the sidha-yoni-asana position may produce heat and even cause orgasm because of the pressure above and below the clitoris.*

A change in the direction of the sexual energy current from a downward and outward movement to an upward and inward movement enriches the brain and strengthens it sufficiently to receive "illumination." People who experience this phenomenon are called *Urdhvaraita* in Sanskrit and they are considered to be successful yogis who have achieved "release."

Kundalini exercise for men

* Naked, perform the microcosmic cycle in a meditative state while storing ki energy in the hara region.

* Rub your hands together, and when they are warm, massage and gently shake your kidneys up to 20 times. Stop and feel the heat.

* Feel that you are inhaling through your kidneys and exhaling ki into the kidney point.

* Repeat the process two to four times. Be aware of the energy link between your kidneys and your genitals.

* Warm your hands again by rubbing them together.

* Gently hold your testicles in one hand, without pressing them, and cover them with your other hand. Now massage your testicles up to 40 times and then feel the accumulation of ki in them.

* While you are holding your testicles in your left hand, place your right hand on your hara.

* Massage your navel with your right hand in a clockwise direction 20 times.

* Produce heat by rubbing your hands together, and then change your position so that you are holding your testicles in your right hand. Massage the hara with your left hand in a counter-clockwise direction about 40 times.

* Cover your penis with both hands, feel the arousal in it, and collect ki by contracting your muscles.

* Stop and be aware of the spread of the energy.

* Hold your right hand above your testicles and your left hand above the Anahata chakra.

* Feel the presence of universal love and draw the energy into your heart.

* Return the energy to the hara by continuing the microcosmic cycle and conclude the exercise by grounding.

The details of the exercise for men are expanded in the exercise for women, and its advantages for men are the same as the ones listed there. Moreover, men are cured of premature ejaculation, prostate problems and other sexual difficulties, and their genitals are strengthened.

The inversion of sexual energy can turn the person into an *Urdhvaraita* and provides perfect release. The person achieves inner tranquillity, heightened creativity and mental awareness, spiritual growth and freedom from disease.

Exercise for linking kundalini for women

The *hoi-yin* position links the meridian of conception to the governor meridian in the upper and lower parts of your body.

* Apply *Mulbandha* by contracting the vaginal and anal muscles. If you contract your anus as if pulling your rectum upward into your body, the vaginal muscle will contract with it automatically.
* Now contract your vaginal muscle as if trying to stop the flow of urine.
* It is important to know that this is also the way to stimulate orgasm. You may feel as if air is coming in through your rectum.
* Maintain this position for as long as you can and then release it.

Repeat the process three times. It may be difficult initially, but with practice you will be able to remain in this position for longer and longer periods of time.

Exercise for linking kundalini for women and men

The *hoi-yin* position links the meridian of conception with the governor meridian in the upper and lower parts of your body.

* Sit in the *sidhasana* position (for men) or the *sidha-yoni-asana* position (for women) and locate the point between your anus and your genitals. This is the Muladhara chakra or the acupuncture point that is called CV-I (conception vessel I). In Chi-Kong, it is called "the gate of life and death."

* Apply *Khechri-mudra* by placing your tongue on your hard palate, right behind your teeth. This action links the meridian of conception and the governor meridian at the upper end of the body, just as the contraction of the perineum does in the root region.

* Touch your palate with the tip of your tongue and hold it in this place for the duration of the exercise.

* The *hoi-yin* position is maintained simultaneously with your tongue touching your hard palate and holding your breath for two to three minutes, during which time you transmit your Reiki tunings.

The aim of this exercise is muscle control. Ki begins to flow upward along the hara line, and cannot flow downward. A link to the earth energy is created by drawing this energy upward into the hara.

Maintaining the *hoi-yin* position and letting the tip of your tongue touch your hard palate creates a closed circuit, and the meridian of conception and the governor meridian are joined at both ends. The microcosmic cycle begins to operate almost immediately.

Ki begins to move downward from the crown chakra and upward from the earth. The hara is activated, and energy moves in the body as if it is creating the figure 8.

Pay attention to the three parts of *hoi-yin* and see that you apply them: contracting the vaginal and anal muscles, placing the tongue on the hard palate, and deep breathing. That is what makes the microcosmic cycle possible.

Version for men

While you are sitting in the *sidhasana* position, apply *Mulbandha* by contracting your anal muscle, placing the tip of your tongue on your hard palate and holding a deep breath for as long as possible – while it is comfortable.

Both men and women must practice the exercises morning and evening. In time, with the performance of the exercises, a good feeling and sound health are consolidated and become a part of everyday life. Advantages that were mentioned previously begin to be evident.

The first exercise is meant for removing energetic blockages, for enhancing spiritual awareness and for developing the body-mind-spirit connection. The second exercise is meant for transmitting Reiki tunings.

That concludes the practice section of Kundalini yoga.

Essential Tantric Reiki points

General Tantric Reiki massage is the starting point for Tantric Reiki for Lovers. After the general massage, and sometimes unrelated to it, we move on to specific massage - both for increasing the effect in particular fields that suit the purpose of the massage, and for overcoming problems and obstacles.

In Tantric Reiki for Lovers, this specific massage includes massaging areas in which the essential points are located - reiki is directed purposely toward the sexual organs according to the Tantric Reiki tradition. Specific massage in Tantric Reiki for Lovers can also take the form of a general feathering of the entire body, or any other massage technique - wherever your imagination takes you!

After the massage, we move on to Tantric Reiki which is based on pressures. To this end, we have to be familiar with 24 essential points in the body. These points are effective during love-making, as well as for relieving menstrual cramps and other pains and symptoms that accompany the monthly period, impotence, premature ejaculation, and so on.

1. The "Intersection of the Three Yins" Tantric Reiki point:

This point is effective in relieving menstrual cramps, period pains, and various emotional and physical symptoms that occur several days before - as well as during - it.

This point is located four finger-widths above the inner ankle bone, behind the tibia (the inner calf bone) on both legs. Vertical pressure is applied to this point with the thumb on the point, and the fingers serving as supports. Pressure should be applied gradually, from light to medium, keeping the thumb on the point for seven seconds, and gradually releasing the pressure without detaching the thumb from the point. The procedure should be repeated several times.

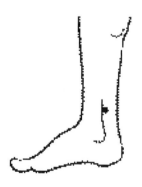

2. The "Sea of Blood" Tantric Reiki point:

This important point, which is located above the knee, on the inner side of both legs, serves to fortify women generally, and to relieve menstrual symptoms, cramps, pains, and fluctuations in their emotional state a few days before as well as during the period.

Pressure is applied to this point while the woman is seated on a chair. Her partner covers her kneecap with his hand. The point is located below his thumb, when he is sitting on the floor (or on a cushion) in front of her. Pressure is applied gradually, keeping the thumb on the point for several seconds, and gradually releasing the pressure without detaching the thumb from the point. The procedure should be repeated.

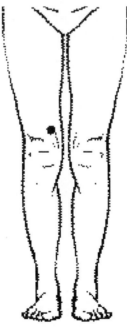

3. The "Original Chi" Tantric Reiki point:

This important point, which fortifies the body in general, and has many therapeutic advantages, is located in the middle of the abdomen, at a distance of three finger-widths above the big bone that is situated above the pubic bone. Using the thumb or forefinger, gentle pressure is applied gradually, keeping the finger on the point for five to ten seconds, and gradually releasing the pressure without detaching the finger from the point. The procedure should be repeated several times.

Besides being an important point for strengthening the body in general, it also serves to relieve menstrual cramps, as well as other pains and symptoms that accompany the monthly cycle. It also provides relief during the mid-life crisis of men, by providing them with psychological encouragement and overall reinforcement.

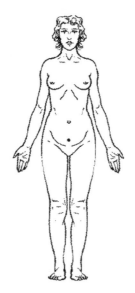

4. The "Walking Three Miles" Tantric Reiki point:

This point is located at a distance of four finger-widths below the kneecap (while sitting on a chair) on both legs. It is located exactly where the fourth finger encounters the tibia, that is, on the edge of the bone toward the inner part of the leg. With fingers enveloping the kneecap, gradual pressure is applied with the thumb, keeping it on the point, and gradually releasing the pressure without detaching the thumb from the point.

The procedure should be repeated several times.

This point is very important, and is also used for general strengthening, and for relieving menstrual pains and cramps as well as other symptoms that accompany the monthly cycle. It also provides relief during the mid-life crisis of men, and fortifies them generally.

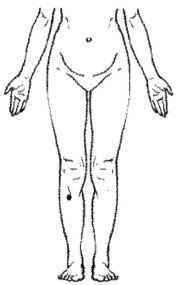

5. The "Pass Organ" Tantric Reiki point:

This important point strengthens the body in general, increases virility, improves sexual performance, and increases sexual arousal during intercourse. It is an excellent point for daily practice in order to improve general sexual functioning.

It is located in the center of the abdomen, just below the navel. Gentle pressure can be applied gradually with the thumb, the forefinger, or the top joint of the forefinger reinforced by the middle finger in order to increase the pressure, keeping the finger on the point for five to ten seconds, and gradually releasing the pressure without detaching the finger from the point. The procedure should be repeated three to five times.

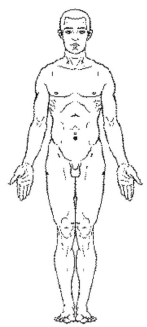

6. The "Middle Extreme" Tantric Reiki point:

In daily practice, pressure on this point helps to increase sexual vigor and to improve sexual function. When pressure is applied to it during foreplay, it is extremely arousing. The point is located in the center of the slope of the abdomen, directly above the pubic bone. There is only one "Middle Extreme" point in the body.

Gentle pressure can be applied gradually with the thumb, the forefinger, or the top joint of the forefinger reinforced by the middle finger in order to increase the pressure, keeping the finger on the point for several seconds, and gradually releasing the pressure without detaching the finger from the point. The procedure should be repeated several times.

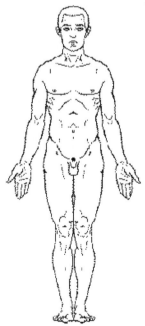

7. The "Crooked Bone" Tantric Reiki point:

This point is located at a distance of two finger-widths above the "Middle Extreme" point. Gentle pressure is applied gradually with the thumb, the forefinger, or the top joint of the forefinger reinforced by the middle finger in order to increase the pressure, keeping the finger on the point for several seconds, and gradually releasing the pressure without detaching the finger from the point.

The procedure should be repeated several times.

In daily practice, pressure on this point serves to improve general sexual functioning, to enhance and fortify sexual vigor, and to increase arousal during foreplay.

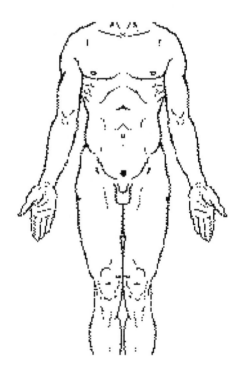

8. The "Conception Vessel" *Tantric Reiki point:*

This point actually consists of several points, which are also known as perineal points, the most important of which is the perineal or "Conception Vessel One" point. These are the most important points in erotic stimulation and for treating various kinds of sexual problems. The "Conception Vessel" meridian is located along the central line of the lower abdomen, and along it are the five most important points for sexual arousal. They can be used for foreplay preceding intercourse, or for strengthening and balancing the sexual system on a daily basis. The points begin from

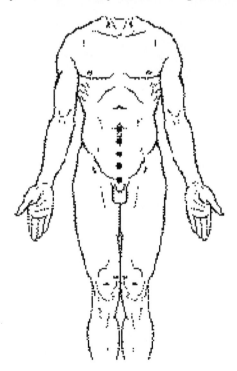

the pubic bone, along the central line, and ascend to a distance of two finger-widths above the navel. Pressure can be applied to the points with the forefinger or the palm.

However, the point that is considered the most significant for sexual arousal during foreplay and intercourse is the one that is located between the anus and the genitals - male or female. Its Chinese name is "Hui Yin," or "The Meeting Point of Feminine Power," and it is extremely powerful from the point of view of the sexual arousal it causes.

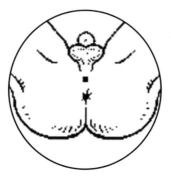

9. The pressure Tantric Reiki point
below the knee:

This pressure point is located below the knee, slightly in the direction of the inner side of the leg. It is very effective in relieving menstrual cramps, as well as other pains and symptoms that accompany the monthly period. Pressure should be applied to this point with the thumb for a few seconds. The point is located on both legs.

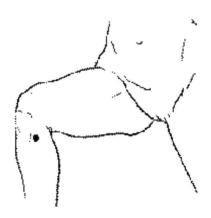

10. The pressure Tantric Reiki point at the base of the calf:

This pressure point is located at the base of the calf on both legs, on its lowest part, and on the inner side of the leg, at a distance of about four finger-widths above the ankle, close to the tibia, but not on it. It is very easy to apply "pinching" pressure to this point, but pressure can also be applied with the forefinger, or with the top joint of the forefinger reinforced by the middle finger in order to increase the pressure, keeping the finger on the point for about seven seconds, and gradually releasing the pressure without detaching the finger from the point. The procedure should be repeated several times.

If pressure is applied to this point on a daily basis, all aspects of sexual function will improve considerably. It helps increase sexual vigor, and when pressure is applied to it during intercourse, it augments and intensifies the sexual experience. In addition, it has a general fortifying effect on the body. Another important action is its ability to relieve menstrual cramps, as well as other pains and symptoms that accompany the monthly period.

11. The pressure Tantric Reiki point on the outer side of the calf:

This pressure point is located at a distance of three finger-widths below the kneecap on both legs, in the direction of the outer side of the calf, close to the tibia, but not on it. Pressure is applied to the point in a sitting position, with the hand covering the kneecap, and the thumb applying the pressure. Pressure is applied gradually several times, keeping the thumb on the point for about five to ten seconds, gradually releasing the pressure without detaching the thumb from the point.

Daily practice on this point improves all aspects of sexual functioning, and increases sexual vigor. Pressure can be applied during intercourse, in order to augment the sexual experience. In addition, this point has an important and varied action for strengthening all the body's functions, and it is very effective for soothing and alleviating inner agitation.

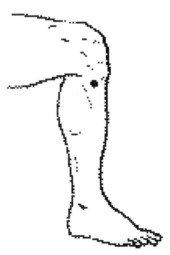

12. The pressure Tantric Reiki point above the knee:

This pressure point is located above the knee, toward the inner part of both legs. This point is also used for relieving menstrual cramps, as well as other pains and symptoms that accompany the monthly period. Pressure is applied by covering the knee with the hand, and the thumb applying gradual pressure, keeping it on the point for seven to ten seconds, and gradually releasing the pressure without detaching the thumb from the point. The procedure is repeated three to five times.

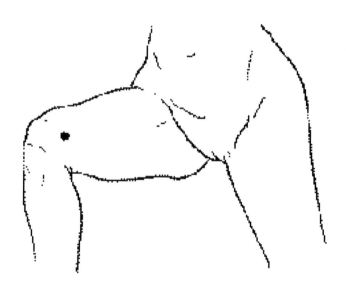

13. The pressure Tantric Reiki point on the outer side of the thigh:

This pressure point is located on the outer side of both thighs, a little in from the crease of the buttocks. This is another point which helps relieve menstrual cramps, as well as other pains and symptoms that accompany the monthly period. Sometimes it is easier to have a partner apply

pressure, when the recipient is standing. Pressure can be applied to the point when the palm is placed at the base of the buttocks, spread out, and the thumb applies gradual pressure to the point, and remains there for about seven seconds. The pressure is released gradually without detaching the thumb from the point. The procedure is repeated at least three times.

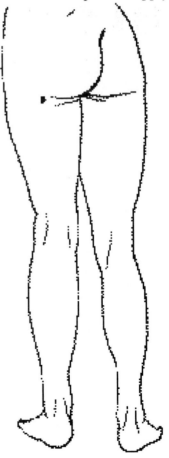

14. The pressure Tantric Reiki point at the top of the bridge of the nose:

This pressure point is located at the top of the bridge of the nose, between the eyebrows. It is used for relieving menopausal symptoms such as hot and cold flashes, backaches, tremors, sudden feelings of exhaustion, and other symptoms. In addition, it helps significantly in alleviating the emotional aspects of men's mid-life crisis. There is only one point like this in the body.

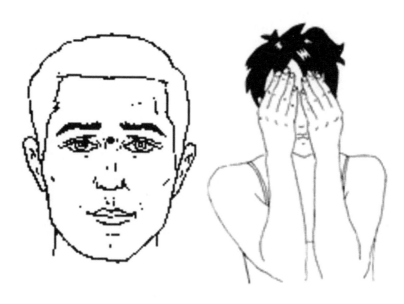

15. The pressure Tantric Reiki point on the sole of the foot:

This pressure point is located between the two pads of the sole of the foot, slightly toward the big toe on both feet. Pressure must be applied to the points on both feet. The point is used for alleviating menopausal symptoms - both physical and emotional.

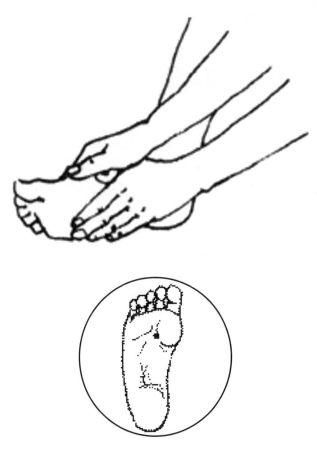

16. The stomach meridian pressure Tantric Reiki points:

One point is located next to the area of the pubic bone (pelvis), and the second below the knee. Pressure is applied to this point for sexual arousal, mainly in cases of frigidity. Despite the distance between the two points, they must both be treated together (if possible), or one after the other.

Note that on each leg, there are two stomach meridian points.

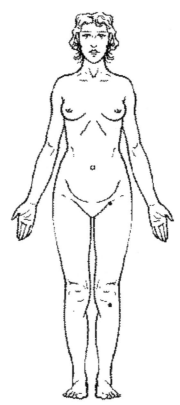

17. The liver meridian pressure Tantric Reiki point:

This pressure point is located on both thighs, slightly below the pelvis in front. (It tends slightly toward the inner part of the thigh.) It serves to increase sexual arousal and helps in cases of frigidity.

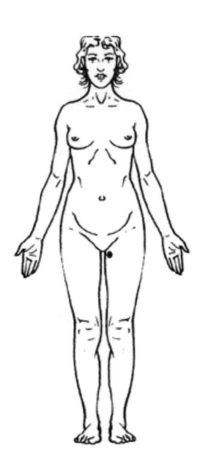

18. The spleen meridian pressure
Tantric Reiki points:

A pair of points: one point is located on the inner part of the leg next to the knee, and the other on the meridian above the ankle. Both of these points help in cases of frigidity. Despite the distance between the two points, they must both be treated together (if possible), or one after the other.

Note that on each leg, there are two spleen meridian points.

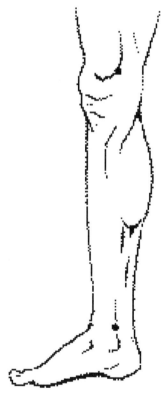

19. The pressure Tantric Reiki points on the back:

There are many pressure points located on the back, and they are connected to the nerves that supply energy to the reproductive organs. These nerves, together with the nerves in the lower back region, control almost all the vital functions of the lower region of the body, such as urination, erection, copulation, and so on. Pressure is applied with the whole palm, preferably with all the fingers simultaneously. In this way, we can treat a large number of points at the same time. Light to medium pressure should be applied, while using all the fingers to apply pressure to the following areas: both sides of the spinal column, right next to the vertebrae, from slightly below the waist down to

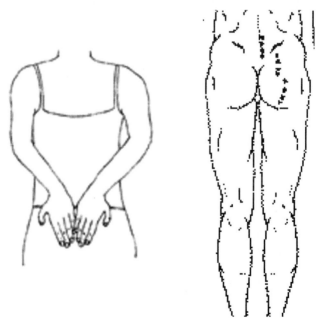

above the end of the coccyx (a palm's length above the coccyx); at a distance of about three finger-widths from this point (when the palm is placed vertically on the area), a bit lower than the first point, again a palm's length; and a third point, at a distance of about three finger-widths (when the hand is held vertically on the body), at a point a bit lower, so that the whole spread hand almost reaches the base of the crease of the buttocks. These important points are extremely effective for increasing sexual arousal.

20. The pressure Tantric Reiki points on the upper thigh:

The pressure points on the thighs, especially at the front of the thighs, are also connected to the kidney, spleen, and other meridians. These points are numerous, and in order to stimulate most of them simultaneously, gentle pressure must be applied to the inner front area of the thighs. In order to stimulate them, it is possible to apply pressure in a variety of ways - by steady pressure, by stroking, or by massage. They are very effective in sexual arousal, and give a new flavor to foreplay. Pressure can also be applied to them during intercourse, in order to intensify the experience.

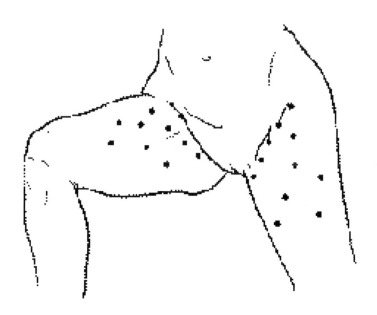

21. The pressure Tantric Reiki points on the ear:

There are numerous nerves on the surface of the outer ear, one of which is connected to the autonomic nervous system, which also plays a role in the various actions of the sexual system. (This particular point is illustrated below. The rest of the points are not indicated.)

Applying pressure to the area of the ear that is parallel to the temple is effective for treating various states of sexual inadequacy, and various problems in sexual functioning. In addition, like the rest of the points on the ear, it also helps increase sexual desire, both during foreplay and generally, when the pressure is applied on a daily basis.

Because of the numerous points in this area, it is a good idea to apply different forms of touch to the ear, such as nibbling on the ear, kissing, sucking, touching, gentle pressure, and so on. Touching the points on the outer ear leads to an increase in sexual arousal and an intensification of the sexual experience, as well as creating stimulation during foreplay. Of course, let's not forget that there are two ears!

22. The pressure Tantric Reiki points on the hand:

The action of this pressure point is widespread and varied, and it reinforces all the functions of the body. It is located on the gap between the thumb and the forefinger on both hands, slightly in the direction of the root of the palm, at a distance of a finger-width below the first joint of the forefinger, on the outer part of the hand, parallel to the bone, but not on it. Pressure should be applied using the "pinching" technique, when the practitioner's forefinger is placed above the pad of the patient's thumb, and pressure is applied with the practitioner's thumb on this point. Both hands should be pressed each time, for a few seconds, and the procedure should be repeated several times without detaching the thumb from the point.

This point serves to fortify and balance the body in general, and daily practice will result in an improvement in all aspects of sexual functioning. The point is also used for increasing sexual vigor, and pressure can be applied to it during intercourse in order to intensify the sexual experience.

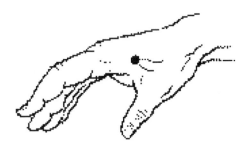

23. The pressure Tantric Reiki point between the eyebrows:

This point is situated exactly between the eyebrows, at the end of the bridge of the nose - not actually on it, but just above it. The bone can be felt below the pressure point. This point is very effective in reducing tension, nervousness, and pressure, and is helpful in relieving headaches. There is one point like this in the body.

Since it is very soothing, it contributes indirectly to increasing the body's vitality and to increasing sexual strength. When pressure is applied to it before intercourse or during foreplay, it increases the enjoyment and the ability to shake off everyday cares, and to concentrate on sexual pleasure. Because of these soothing properties, it is also helpful in cases of loss of libido or a drop in sexual pleasure as a result of tension or anxiety.

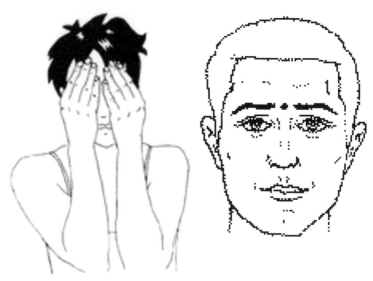

Pressure can be applied to this point with the thumb, but it is easier to use the forefinger or the middle finger. It is also possible to apply pressure with the top joint of the forefinger reinforced by the middle finger to increase the pressure. Gradual pressure should be applied to the point, keeping the finger on the point for a few seconds, and gradually releasing the pressure without detaching the finger from the point. The procedure should be repeated several times.

24. The pressure Tantric Reiki point between the upper lip and the nose:

This point is situated in the indentation between the upper lip and the nose. It helps considerably in releasing tensions and pressures, and in attaining a state of calmness and serenity. In addition, it is known as a point that contributes to the stimulation of facial beauty and the skin of the face. There is one point like this in the body.

Gradual, gentle pressure should be applied to this point, and the pressure should be released gradually without detaching the finger from the point. The procedure should be repeated several times.

By means of its soothing action, this point helps increase sexual power, enjoyment during intercourse, and the ability to concentrate on sexual pleasure. Moreover, it helps increase the body's vitality. It is recommended for use in various problems of a decrease in libido and sexual arousal, which are linked to the psychological aspects of anxiety and tension.

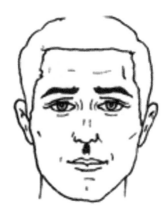

These 24 Tantric Reiki points are the central points in Tantric Reiki for Lovers.

Note that some of the points are close to each other - for example, number 23 is close to and above number 14; numbers 1-10 are very close together, and so on. As a result, when we apply pressure to one point, we sometimes activate the point that is close to it. This is not in the least harmful.

Tantric Reiki for Lovers

Up to this point, you have become familiar with the fundamentals of *Tantric Reiki*, the meridians, and the pressure points, and you have learned a great deal about massage (including massage with oils) and pressures. You are now no doubt conversant with the massage and pressure techniques, as well as with the location of the 24 most important "sexual" points in *Tantric Reiki* for Lovers.

Although we have presented the subject in general, there is a certain degree of repetition of what has already been written (mainly in the elaboration on the points and the explanation of the erotic massage) in the descriptions of *Tantric Reiki* for Lovers.

Now we will move on to the second part of the book, in which we will focus on *Tantric Reiki* for Lovers. In this part, we will present the preferred pressures for *Tantric Reiki* for Lovers, we will examine several problems and conditions that require special treatment, and we will prepare ourselves for the piece de resistance in the third part, which includes true stories about the wonders of *Tantric Reiki* for Lovers.

I will take it for granted that you are familiar with what appeared in the first part of the book, and so from now on I will use mainly the names of the pressures, without going into detail about what has already been described. Every term that appears from here on is explained in the first part of the book.

Unique pressure techniques in Tantric Reiki for Lovers

In *Tantric Reiki* for Lovers, there are two groups of pressure techniques. The first is used during sexual intercourse, and constitutes part of the foreplay and the love-making itself. The second is used to stimulate and accumulate sexual vigor.

In the second technique, the effect is cumulative, as the technique is applied on a daily basis, or several times a week, in order to arouse, balance, and stimulate sexual vitality and vigor, and to solve various sexual problems. This technique is not directly connected to love-making, and can be self-applied, even though it is always preferable for the other member of the couple to apply the pressures.

The *Tantric Reiki* pressure techniques from the first group are applied during foreplay, during the sexual act, and after it, and their aim is to be part of the actual love-making. The pressure techniques increase and intensify pleasure during foreplay, and prepare the body for orgasmic release, as well as increase and intensify the orgasm itself.

They are extremely important when the couple's sex life tends to be boring, routine, or unsatisfying, or when there are specific problems in sexual functioning. Later on, we will focus on these points. Remember that there are points whose purpose is to strengthen and arouse sluggish libido, and, conversely, there are points that help to tone down excessive libido.

The advantage of *Tantric Reiki* for Lovers is that it does not require physical strength, and every normal person can apply the pressures very easily. In addition to the physical aspect of the pressure points, they contribute to the closeness and psychological awakening of the couple. It is recommended that even if only one member of the couple suffers from any kind of sexual problem, both members pleasure each other with *Tantric Reiki* pressures. The effect of mutually applied pressures, whether during intercourse or separately from it, is powerful, extending beyond the actual stimulation of the points. The pressures teach people how to touch each other and discover what kind of touch the other person enjoys and finds pleasurable; it helps people know and accept their own body and that of their partner, and helps eliminate the barriers, inhibitions, and psychological fears that people have concerning sexual relations.

Practicing applying the pressures is very simple, and everyone can do it, alone or in couples. The location of the pressure points is identical in men and in women, but varies relative to the physical build of each individual, depending on size and height.

Locating the points is very easy, but remember that locations such as "four finger-widths" or "a palm's length" refer to the patient's body - that is, the person who is receiving the *Tantric Reiki*. Therefore, when you set out to apply pressures to your partner, you must measure the points according to the width or length of his/her fingers.

The strength of the pressure to be applied is medium - neither too strong nor too weak - and you should press until just before it hurts; however, you must not reach the point of pain. In the case of a person who is overweight, the pressure should be slightly greater, in order to reach the points. In the case of an especially thin person, the pressure should be lighter and more superficial. As a person gets older, the sensitivity of his nerves in certain places diminishes, which means that these points need greater stimulation. You should not press too hard, but you should press for a longer time in order to ensure the correct and optimal stimulation of the point.

The pressures

In *Tantric Reiki* for Lovers, we mainly use the four pressures that are detailed here, as well as a small or large variety of massage techniques that precede or combine with the pressures.

It is a good idea to practice these pressures - especially on oneself, in order to feel the sensation and learn the degree of strength necessary for each pressure.

Thumb pressure:

The most convenient and effective form of pressure is that applied with the thumb. By means of this pressure, it is possible to use a great deal of strength, and to press deeply into the flesh.

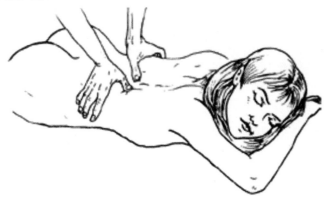

It is important to ensure that your fingernails are short before applying the pressure, since, during a vertical thumb pressure, which is the most effective, long fingernails are liable to hurt your partner.

Finger pressure:

Another form of pressure is that applied with the forefinger or middle finger. Since the pressure applied by these fingers is not great, you can press with your forefinger while reinforcing it with your middle finger, which is pressing on the top joint of the forefinger.

"Pinching" pressure:

In certain regions of the body, it is easier to apply pinching pressure. This does not mean actual pinching with the fingers, but rather a "pinch" with the whole palm, or with some of the fingers, in order to grasp the place where the point is located.

This technique can be applied to a particular point in order to increase the thumb pressure, or to press more steadily with the thumb. In such a case, most of the strength of the pressure must be transferred to the thumb.

It is preferable to use this technique only in cases where it is not possible to use only the thumb - for instance, when pressing the sides of the ankle, or certain points on the palm. In any case, the pressure is applied by the thumb, which is the main "presser" in this technique, while the fingers serve as counter-supports.

Applying pressure using the pads of the palms:

This pressure is used when you need to press on a larger area, on two or more points simultaneously, or on an area that contains a large number of points very close to one another.

In this technique, your palms are placed parallel to each other on the center of the area, and the pressure of your

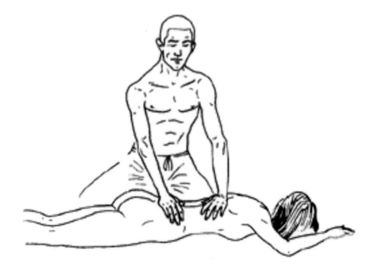

body is channeled into the pads of the palms. This form of pressure creates a strong, steady pressure on the points.

The pressures must be applied gradually, up to just before the point where the person begins to feel a little pain. This is when the pressure should cease, and the finger should be held on the point for between five and ten seconds.

After this, the pressure exerted by the finger should be gradually reduced, until the finger is touching the point without any pressure.

Remember that you must not jab the point suddenly and quickly, or release the finger abruptly. Everything should be done slowly and gradually. When your finger is touching the point without pressure, you must wait about five seconds, and then, without detaching it from the point, gradually begin to apply pressure again. This procedure should generally be repeated three times before moving on to the next point.

During the pressure, do not rotate your finger or thumb, or "dig" with them, or perform massaging movements. The pressure must be direct and steady.